CW00983963

77 Social Media Tips for Business

I.G. Media Marketing.
26 Royce Close,
Yaxley,
Peterborough, PE7 3QY

ISBN 978-1-4477-6297-3 (get this from Lulu)

Disclaimer

This book has been written to provide information about Internet marketing. Every effort has been made to make this book as complete and accurate as possible. However, there may be mistakes in typography or content. Also, this book provides information on Internet marketing only up to the publishing date. Therefore, this book should be used as a guide -not as the ultimate source of Internet marketing information.

The purpose of this book is to educate. The author and the publisher do not warrant that the information contained in this book is fully complete and shall not be responsible for any errors or omissions. The author and publisher shall have neither liability nor responsibility to any person or entity with respect to any loss or damage caused or alleged to be caused directly or indirectly by this book.

Table of Contents

About Ian

I'm Ian Gibbins the owner of I.G. Media Marketing. I first became involved with internet marketing in 2009 and soon discovered a passion for how businesses could use social media to promote themselves along with their products and services through the conversations and interaction that takes place naturally across the networks.

I have received many requests from business owners to create social media marketing campaigns for them, and I have had the pleasure of working with some wonderful, forward thinking companies as close to home as Peterborough and as far afield as Dubai.

I now specialise in this area of social media marketing, along with coaching on a 1-2-1 or group basis, and also through running workshops and speaking events around the UK.

I believe there has never been a better time in history for communicating as effectively with each other as there is today, and it is the social media networks that provide us with the tools to enable us to achieve this.

Introduction

The rise of social media has transformed business as we once knew it. In the past, business owners were limited in how they interacted with customers, how they collected information about them, and how they marketed new products and services to them. Today, these strictures have been removed, permitting business owners to gather information, learn, and respond much faster than ever before.

It has also transformed the business landscape in another way: by creating a rift between those who know how to navigate social media sites and services; and those who do not. Those who don't know how to use social media services may find themselves on the defensive constantly-doing anything to retain customers -even if they had successful business model only years ago. On the other hand, those who feel comfortable with social media may now find themselves at a significant advantage.

Whether you're currently using social media to promote your business or are thinking about doing so, it is important for you to understand how to do it correctly. No matter whether you're inexperienced or a veteran social marketer, if you don't have the right information, it can be easy to botch a marketing campaign or simply run out of ideas.

Fortunately for you, this guide was designed for people in your exact position: those who know that social media is an important part of doing business today; and who want to learn how to use it correctly.

In the rest of this guide, I'm going to provide you with 77 stand-alone tips that you can use to integrate social media into your business, use it to market your products, use it to find new customers, and use it to manage existing customers and extract information from them.

To your online success!

Ian.

#1: Present a Consistent Social Media Identity

Now that you're ready to enter the world of social media, it's important for you to spend some time carefully thinking about your social media identity before you create a Twitter account, launch a Facebook fan page, and begin to market your business through social media channels.

The first thing you will want to do is decide whether you should market your business as your business, as yourself, or as both. Each of the three options has benefits, but it is ultimately up to you to decide which will work best for your particular situation.

Once you have selected your route, you should create accounts on social media sites and setup a profile that reflects your choice. For instance, a Twitter account for your business should focus exclusively on business activities—and not your personal life.

#2: Create a Coherent Social Media Message

This tip closely relates to tip #1: once you have your social media site profiles setup, you'll want to start finding followers; and then using those followers to collect information and market products.

As you go through this process, it is important to maintain a coherent message. For this reason, it might make sense to spend some time planning a general "theme" for your social media profiles. For instance, is their purpose to alert people to sales and to tell them about contests you are holding? Or is the purpose to discuss the general industry in which your business falls; and mention your new products casually?

There's not necessarily a best approach to take here, but it is important that you pick one and stick with it. Creating an incoherent message and confuse and drive away potential customers who are following you.

#3: Create a Twitter Profile

Once you have setup your Twitter account, it is critical that you spend some time to personalize your profile. Most businesses that do not do this will be perceived as spammers when they ask Twitter users to follow them.

When it comes to setting up a personalized profile on Twitter, there's not much to do. All you have to do is select a pre-existing background (or create a customized one), select your avatar thumbnail photo, and then fill in some short "bio" and "about me" information.

As far as your avatar goes, it is probably a good idea to use the logo for your business; and it may also be a good idea to create a custom background that also includes your logo.

Finally, remember to add the URL of your business; and to create a bio section that briefly explains 1) what your business does; and 2) what the purpose of this Twitter profile is (i.e. to give away free stuff, to hold contests, or to provide free information).

#4: Create a Page for Your Business on Facebook

Facebook is one of the most promising social media outlets when it comes to marketing your products. One good way to use Facebook is to create a business page on the site; and to use it to draw in potential buyers.

Start by investing some time to create a high-quality page. This page should include links to your site, a well-written description of what you do, and a brief description of the purpose of your page (i.e. to provide all of your loyal customers with free information about upcoming product launches, product give-aways, and coupons).

If you don't yet have enough "fans" to get the ball rolling, it might make sense to start by giving people an incentive to become a fan. You could do something like this: offer everyone who joins your page a free report, or a 20% off coupon for one of your products.

#5: Track Your Twitter Results

As with any marketing campaign, you should monitor your Twitter promotional campaigns by tracking the results. One free way to do this is to use http://search.Twitter.com/ to find all instances of people talking about you or your business on Twitter.

Another tool you can use is called tweet Beep: http://tweetbeep.com/. This service will automatically email you whenever something about you or your business is tweeted.

Finally, you can check your website's analytics/traffic statistics program to determine how much traffic you have received from Twitter. If you don't currently have a good traffic statistics program, you can get one for free from here: http://www.statcounter.com/.

#6: Think in Terms of Social Capital

When it comes to using any form of social media services to promote your business, it is always a good idea to think in terms of building social capital that will generate flows of returns over a long period of time.

It's important to understand this because many marketers treat social media sites like pay-per-click (PPC) advertising services. That is—they expect to see returns immediately after creating an account on Facebook or Twitter.

In reality, using social media sites correctly requires that you build up a large following over a long period of time. You can think of these networks that you are building as a form of capital. Once sufficiently large, you can begin to use it to bring in additional members (without actively marketing) and additional customers.

#7: Use the Twitter Search Engine

Another approach you can take is to use the Twitter search engine to find tweets related to your business's niche. This is an easy way to locate people who might be interested in your products or services.

Once you have located some tweets related to your niche, you can follow them back to the source, determine whether the person involved might be interested in your niche, and then invite them to follow you if so.

Initially, a lot of people you add may opt not to follow you; however, over time, if you accumulate 50 new followers each day, you'll gain momentum. If you make interesting tweets, offer coupons, or tweet vital information, you might get re-tweeted, expanding your reach and possibly bringing in new followers.

#8: Use Twitter to Conduct Market Research

Unfortunately, marketers often approach social media with the wrong attitude. They hope that by simply creating a Twitter account, adding every person who is willing to follow them, and spamming blatantly commercial messages, they'll make money. In fact, this is one of the worst ways to make money with a social network, as potential buyers will see through it easily; and will choose to opt out.

On the other hand, marketers often miss the great opportunities that Twitter presents—such as doing market research. In the past, it was very hard to observe your customers when they talked casually about your products or about competing products; however, this is exactly what you can do with Twitter (perhaps by using the Twitter Search Engine, as mentioned above).

#9: Create a Tutorial Series on YouTube

Many business owners are using video marketing today with huge success, and with YouTube now being the 2nd largest search engine, let's face it if you are not utilising their service then you are missing out on a huge amount of traffic to your website.

So, to begin with, I personally suggest that you start by creating a tutorial series. This could be something like 5 videos, each of which covers a topic in an area related to your business.

If the videos are well-made; and if you market them well to get the ball rolling, there's a good chance you could see a viral effect, where others begin referring friends to your videos without any compensation for doing so.

#10: Create a LinkedIn Profile

If you're not familiar with LinkedIn, you might be surprised to find out that they've already collected information about you; and have used it to construct a profile that might include some or all of the following information:

1) where you went to college;
2) what jobs you hold or have held in the past;
3) what businesses you have owned or own;
4) high-level personal and professional information about you.

If you want to control what that profile says; and to use it to network with other business owners and potential clients, it's a good idea to start by creating a profile. Once you do that, you have a lot of options in terms of promotion and networking; however, for now, simply worry about getting the ball rolling by creating a profile.

#11: Put a Thumbnail Photo in Your Profiles

No matter what social network you are using, it's always a good idea to place a thumbnail photo of yourself (or at least your business's logo) where possible. In general, people will be hesitant to interact with profiles that don't have faces attached to them.

Of course, this is a personal decision and is ultimately up to you; however, if you plan to take your social network marketing efforts seriously, this is an important step to take.

#12: Post Free Information

As I've mentioned before, one of the best approaches you can take to social media marketing is to disarm potential followers by providing something truly useful. For instance, you could provide free information about something related to your niche.

You could provide:

1. Links to important news related to your niche
2. Commentaries on important happenings within your niche
3. Links to sales and coupons (even if they're not your own)

Once you use these strategies to build rapport with your visitors, you can then begin to reap the rewards by marketing various products to them.

#13: Promote Through Blog-Commenting

Many marketers believe that the only way to get traffic to a blog is to post frequently, ping, and optimize for natural search engine traffic. In fact, one of the greatest ways to generate traffic via blogs doesn't involve any of this.

The approach I'm talking about is simple: get direct traffic from other blogs by commenting frequently. Of course, it's important to understand that when I say "comment frequently," I don't mean spam other people's blogs with irrelevant information. Rather, I simply mean that you should look for relevant conversions in niche blogs; and then make a useful, intelligent comment that links back to your blog.

If you spend a lot of time making useful comments, there's a good chance you'll re-direct some of the traffic that lands on the big name blogs to your own. You can then pass this traffic through the sales funnel.

#14: Encourage Customers to Use Your Page

There are two benefits of encouraging existing customers to become a fan of your business on Facebook. The first is that you can slowly move away from paid mediums (such as reliance bulk mail and autoresponders to disseminate important information to customers.

The second major benefit is that you can market new products and services to existing customers without pitching to them directly. You can do this by simply creating a status update on Facebook. Whenever they log into their account (even if they have no interest in conducting business), they'll see your status update on their feed. If they find what you're offering useful, they might just buy.

The best part of all of this is that you didn't have to make a high-pressure sales pitch, which might be awkward to do with existing clients. Instead, you can simply let them choose which pitches interest them; and which do not.

#15: Use Your Own Judgment Over Experts

Of course, you might now be asking whether or not you should follow this tip, since I'm suggesting that you follow your own intuition, rather than my advice; however, in all seriousness, when it comes to building your brand online through social marketing devices, it is important that you think about your own business, rather than the generic business that experts have in mind when they write guides like this.

If you read something that conflicts with the type of brand you want to create for your business, then you should go with your own thoughts, rather than misapplying advice that may be useful for other business models—but not your own.

#16: Improve Your LinkedIn Search Ranking

One of the best uses of Linkedin.com is to generate organic search engine traffic related to your niche. How can you do this? By getting your customers to review you on Linkedin.com. With each positive review, your profile's search engine ranking position will improve.

This can do two things for you:

1) It can direct people looking for products related to your niche to your linkedin.com profile; and

2) It can get more people to find your website through your profile.

In either case, you have the potential to capture a great deal of extra traffic from individuals who are highly-targeted; and who are already interested in purchasing a product or service in your niche.

#17: Integrate Social Media Marketing Efforts

Rather than using your Twitter and Facebook accounts in total isolation from the rest of your business, think about using them as complements. For instance, if you do print advertising, you might consider using it to channel traffic to your social networking site profiles.

For instance, it has become common on news channels to refer watchers to company (and reporter) Facebook profiles and Twitter profiles. The reason for this is simple: by getting people to follow them through social networking sites, those news stations gain yet another point through which they can advertise and engage watchers.

If you use this strategy correctly, you could significantly boost the results from your other marketing campaigns by filtering visitors through your network. This will allow you to capture visitors by getting them to join your network, so that you can repeatedly pitch to them (rather than only once) in a low-pressure atmosphere.

#18: Use Forums to Pull in Site Visitors

Forums make up one of the oldest segments of social networking sites on the Internet. If you're like most people, you probably "lurk" on a few forums; and possibly post on a few yourself, too.

Forums offer great potential when it comes to capturing visitors for your site. It's important to keep in mind, though, that all the usual social marketing rules are still in force when it comes to forums.

For instance, just as you wouldn't make shameless pitches on Facebook, you also shouldn't do that on forums. Instead, you should approach them by posting useful information; and then sending readers to your site via a signature at the bottom of each post.

This makes things each for you by helping you avoid high-pressure sales situations; and if you do it correctly, it can be one of the easiest and most profitable ways to draw in new customers.

#19: Link Up with Seasoned Experts

When it comes to social networks, there are usually influential individuals who have hundreds or thousands of friends/followers; and who many people pay attention to. Of course, there are movie stars and politicians who tweet, but I don't mean these people in particular. Rather, identify the important people in your niche who use Linkedin.com, Facebook.com, Twitter.com, and other social networks. Become friends with these people; and then solicit their help in discrete ways.

Again, the same principle applies that I mentioned before: instead of directly pitching to them, make them pay attention to you by providing useful information and insightful commentary. On Twitter, this might buy you an influential retweet; and in the blogosphere, this might buy you a link to your site from a high-traffic blog. Whatever you do, don't try to spam the influential people you contact. They probably receive hundreds of similar pitches; and have grown accustomed to simply ignoring them, so don't expect them to do different for you.

#20: Remember Social Media Marketing is Still Marketing

At the end of the day, your goal for all social media projects should be to earn some type of return. Now, this return might not be immediate; and it may even take months or even a year to realize. But with that said, your goal should still be a return.

With that in mind, think about how you can make your social media marketing ventures more profitable. One way you can do this is to cut down on the amount of time you spend doing things that aren't profitable.

For instance, on a daily basis, you might receive Facebook friend requests, Twitter follower requests, and other requests; however, rather than processing each one as it becomes available, you should think about doing it on a weekly (or at least daily basis).

Alternatively, you might consider using social networking sites with your phone. This will allow you to make requests, accept requests, and perform updates when you have free time, but are not near a computer.

#21: Join Networks Related to Your Niche

Aside from the large networks, such as Facebook, LinkedIn and Twitter, there are smaller niche networks. For instance, there is a social network exclusively for real estate professionals. There are also networks for Internet marketing, aviation, golf, and virtually any topic you can imagine.

One of the biggest benefits to joining these niche networks is that everyone on them is a potential customer. This is especially true if you sell business-to-business products or services.

Again, all the same rules apply if you plan to use these niche sites. Don't spam members with commercial advertisements, but instead, try to offer something that is truly valuable for free; and then use that to draw in other members and to eventually sell them your products.

#22: Link Your Twitter and Facebook Accounts

One way to save some time while maintaining your presence on both Facebook and Twitter, is to link the two accounts. This will allow you to have Facebook automatically update your status using your tweets.

Doing this is pretty simple; and can save you the hassle of moving between the two accounts and re-posting the same message multiple times. If this sounds like a good idea to you, go to the following URL: http://apps.facebook.com/Twitter/.

Once you're there, all you have to do is click the button to allow Twitter to post your tweets to your Facebook account. After that, your tweets will automatically be posted to your Facebook account.

#23: Give a Behind-the-Scenes Tour

One of the great things about being able to interact so freely with your customer base is that you can extract important information from them. Another benefit is that you can send them important signals about your business.

For instance, one thing you can do through your Facebook page is offer your "fans" a behind-the-scenes look at what goes on with your business on a daily basis. You could use status updates to announce the various stages of a product launch; or you could announce new product ideas you have.

This will do two things for you: 1) it will increase customer engagement by exposing them to your thought process and daily business happenings; and 2) it will show them how much thought and work goes into the products you create, so that they grow to appreciate your brand as a result.

#24: Encourage Others to Promote Your Pages

Earlier, I mentioned that you can use contests and other incentives to get people to become a "fan" or a follower. But even if you don't want to go that far, there are much simpler things that you can do to draw in new members of your network.

For starts, you can encourage people to tell others about your fan page or Twitter account. This is as simple as including 2-3 lines of text on your profile that explicitly state those visitors should tell friends and family about your profile if they find it useful.

#25: Avoid Engaging in Flaming or Fights

Regardless of which form of social media you are using, be it Facebook, Twitter, blogs, or forums, remember that you're always representing your business. Engaging in flame war on a forum; or personally attacking a blog reader is unlikely to bring you good press.

In addition to creating enemies, flaming will also make your business look amateurish; and could cause existing customers to seek out other sources for the products they buy.

#26: Participate in Discussions with Visitors

Unlike most marketing campaigns you've probably run, you can't simply create an ad, purchase ad space somewhere, and then wait for the buyers to come in. It's quite the opposite with social networking sites.

Instead of creating a profile, adding some information, and then waiting for people to buy, you should focus some energy on engaging the people who actually do show up. If they have questions about your business or products, be sure you respond in a timely manner and with thoughtful explanations.

The more you engage your customers, the greater your base of followers will become. At some point, it'll become self-perpetuating, so that your followers bring in new followers on a regular basis. But it all starts with you closely engaging your followers.

#27: Let Customers Contribute to Your Fan Page

One of the most important functions of social media is that it allows businesses and organizations to receive feedback from customers and visitors, which they can then respond to through the various social media services they are using.

You should think of doing this with your Facebook fan page. Consider asking visitors to post or send you a story about how they've used your product. You can then hold a contest where the person who wrote the best story gets free products from your online store.

#28: Show How Your Business Helps Others

Consider doing regular give-aways or charity events. Either give your product to someone who needs it, but cannot afford it; or hold a sale and give a portion of the proceeds to charity.

Doing these acts of charity will not only make you feel good about yourself, but it will also help you to demonstrate what type of person you are to your customers. In their eyes, this will boost the credibility of your business; and may give you an advantage over less socially conscious business owners.

#29: Provide Upset Clients with Compensation

Using the Twitter Search Engine, try to find all instances where your products and services have been mentioned. In particular, look for bad reviews of your products, complaints about customer service, and generally anything else that is negative.

Once you locate these negative comments, make a concerted effort to respond to each of them individually. You can do this by providing those with complaints free products; or by offering to redress the problems they have (if this is possible).

If you find that people are complaining about a certain feature of your product, then you may want to consider fixing it (if it is sufficiently inexpensive)—and then re-releasing it for free to those who have already purchased.

Using the strategies above, you should be able to turn any negative press you find into positive press, as people are likely to say good things about you after you redress the problems or offer compensation.

#30: Remember Your Time Is Valuable

As a business owner, you value your time greatly. You know that every move you make impacts the productivity of the entire business—not just your own. This is why it is so important for you to cautiously make time-allocation decisions.

When it comes to social media marketing, most would argue that you should err on the side of over-engagement, rather than under-engagement. I agree with this; however, I would suggest that you take steps to automate procedures and to engage customers efficiently where you do it.

As I've said earlier, you should treat your social media marketing campaign like a true marketing campaign. If you were wasting an inordinate amount of time across any other dimension with your business (and weren't getting any return from it), you'd either change your approach or find more ways to be efficient with your current approach. And that is exactly what you should do here, too.

#31: Don't Let Privacy Concerns Stifle Your Marketing Campaigns

Many who are new to social media marketing worry that these techniques will expose too much information about their personal lives. While this concern certainly is valid, it is often much less important than people think it will be.

I personally suggest that you don't make worrying about your privacy a top priority. If you are selling products that you are proud of, you shouldn't worry about associating your name and a thumbnail photo of yourself with your products.

Of course, when it comes to giving information like your address or anything else that is deeply personal in nature, it's entirely up to you to determine whether or not it is worth it; however, for minor pieces of personal information, there are good reasons to believe that giving it out will do nothing other than help you.

#32: Don't Live in Fear of Making Mistakes

One common theme that paralyzes social media campaigns is the fear of making mistakes. Often, businesses do not even bother to create a Facebook fan page, a Twitter account, or a blog simply because they believe they may make an embarrassing mistake that reflects poorly on the business.

The more common problem that businesses have is that they're too paralyzed by fear to even build up a fan base to witness such a mistake.

I personally recommend that you work hard to build up your network; and spend less time worrying about making mistakes. If anything, you're more likely to make these mistakes in the early stages of your campaign, which is exactly when the fewest people will be able to observe them (because you won't have many followers).

In short—stop worrying so much about the mistakes. Instead, worry more about how you're going to find more people to follow you.

46

#33: Using Tumblr to Save Time

If you use multiple social networks, it may be a good idea to consolidate your workload, so that you don't spend a large chunk of your time repeating the same tasks. One way in which you can do this is by using http://www.tumblr.com.

Much like the Facebook app I mentioned earlier, Tumblr allows you to post to all of your accounts at one time. This means that you can tweet, post a Facebook status update, and post to any of your other accounts at the same time.

#34: Integrate Twitter with Your Homepage

If you want to make your site more dynamic, you may want to consider adding a scrolling Twitter feed. In brief, this is basically just a script that cycles through all of your tweets, displaying them in sequential order in a nice-looking frame.

This is always a nice touch to add to your site. It will not only improve the appearance of your site, but it will also create the feeling of dynamicity. Visitors will enjoy reading it; and may choose to follow the feed to your Twitter profile, where they can become a follower.

To create such a feed, all you have to do is use a widget like this:

http://www.widgetbox.com/widget/twidget.

It will generate code that you can simply copy-and-paste into your site editor.

#35: Use Tumblr for Longer Tweets

As I've mentioned before, Tumblr can be an incredibly useful tool for businesses who want to want to create a presence in the blogosphere. It can also be used for other things, too.

For instance, if you find that you are often unable to communicate enough information in a 140-character tweet, you may want to consider using Tumblr to tweet instead. This will allow you to write a message of any length; and then allow Tumblr to automatically tweet the first 140 characters of it with a link back to the blog post.

#36: Investigate Blogging Platforms

In addition to its integration with Twitter and Facebook, Tumblr offers other significant benefits—most of which become apparent when you compare it to other blogging platforms.

Of all the benefits Tumblr offers, one of the most important is its simplicity. Going even further than Wordpress, Tumblr offers an extremely basic user interface that allows you to choose between functions such as "text" and "pictures." This can be very important if you want to use Tumblr quickly and move on; however, if you want a more customizable platform, then you may want to consider doing your own programming or using Wordpress.

#37: Select a Tumblr Theme

One important part of using Tumblr correctly is
selecting a clean theme that you can use on your blog.
Since many people who read your tweets for the first
time may end up on your Tumblr page, it is important
to create a good impression quickly. Otherwise, you
risk losing a potential customer before you've had any
time to pitch to her.

One option is simply to select one of the available
Tumblr themes. These are largely clean and
professional; however, it is likely that visitors will have
seen them elsewhere.

Another option is to go to your Tumblr dashboard, and
then click "customize," "theme," and then "use custom
HTML." You can then take HTML code from any site
that offers free Tumblr themes and paste it into the
form.

#38: Consider Alternatives to Tumblr

In the last few tips, I've covered how to use Tumblr exhaustively; however, what I did not mention is that there are a number of good alternatives to Tumblr. If you want to check out these alternatives services, here's where I would suggest you look:

1. http://www.ping.fm. This service is similar to what Tumblr offers in terms of automatic re-posting services. If you want to have your blog posts automatically posted to Twitter and also added to your Facebook status, then you may want to consider using Ping.fm.
2. http://www.wordpress.com. If you're not satisfied with Tumblr's blog interface, then you may want to consider using something like Wordpress.com instead. Similar to Tumblr, the Wordpress user interface is also easy; however, it offers more plugins, themes, and possibilities for customization.

#39: Use Last.fm for Music-Related Businesses

If your business relates to music at all, then it might be a wise idea to employ lesser-known social networking services, such as www.last.fm. If you're not familiar with last.fm, it's a form of Internet radio that automatically creates playlists for you.

As you list to music on the site (or even if you opt to let the site capture the music that you listen to on iTunes or elsewhere), the site records your choices; and then adds them to your last.fm profile, which any user may view. This may sound like a fringe idea, but if you happen to be in the music business or sell "how-to" music products, using last.fm could be a great way to build rapport with your customer base. It will not only show that you're a real person (and not just some mysterious person trying to hammer products down people's throats), but will also tell your customers something about you—what music you like.

#40: Refer From Your Profile to Your Page

When it comes to using Facebook to promote your business, it is almost always a good idea to have both a business/personal profile and a fan page. Doing this gives you a great deal of versatility when it comes to recruiting new fans.

You can use the following approach: first, locate people who could be potential customers for your business. Next, use your business/personal profile to add them as a friend (and hope that they accept).

After you've added the people in question as friends, you can then use Facebook to suggest that they become a fan of your business. Many may ignore or reject this offer; however, some will join and this will add to your fan base. One important thing to note is that you should avoid making the same suggestion to the same friends multiple times. For instance, each time you add a friend, do not suggest that they add other people that you know. Also, do not ask them to join the fan page multiple times.

#41: Utilize Your E-mail List

Once you have both a personal/business page and a
fan page on Facebook, it's time to start recruiting
"fans." Remember: the more fans you have, the more
people you can market to on a recurring basis.
Additionally, the more fans you have, the more fan
referrals you'll get without doing any additional work.

A good place to start when it comes to building a fan
base is to take your email list from your autoresponder.
Before you do anything else, create a spare Gmail
account and add all of your contacts to it.

Next, login your Facebook account and select the
option to locate friends using email addresses. After
you do this, use the option to search from an existing
contact list (and use the Gmail account you just
created). This approach will allow you to quickly
determine whether anyone from your original
autoresponder list was using Facebook; and, if they
were, to add them as a friend.

#42: Refer Your New Friends to Your Page

The previous tip explained how you can quickly locate new friends using the email addresses you have in your autoresponder account; however, it is important that you go beyond simply adding them as a friend to your personal/business profile.

Once they choose to become your friend, you will want to suggest that they become a fan of your business. Again, as I said earlier, avoid spamming them or being pushy. Also, realize that many will decline or ignore your invitation.

It is important for you to take this approach—rather than simply using a fan page —since you will have no means to get your email list contacts to become fans without first become your friend.

#43: Use Email Lists to Find Twitter Customers

Once you setup a Gmail account and copy-over all of your contacts from your autoresponder, you can next consider finding all of your contacts on Twitter. Again, the process will be similar. You will use Twitter to search for each person by email address.

As you find new people, request to follow them. As with Facebook, you'll find that many will not follow you back; however, at least a few will opt to follow you on Twitter, and this could provide a significant boost to your reach.

Overall, when employing this strategy, you should stay focused on growing your list of Twitter followers; and ignore all other objectives for the time being. If you cannot sell people your products immediately, that is okay. Instead, just worry about getting them to follow you.

#44: Put Your Latest Updates in Your RSS Feeds

If you decide to use a service like Tumblr or some other blogging platform, it is critical that you setup an RSS feed. Today, many people do not return to a blog more than once. Instead, they assess it, determine whether it provides high-quality content, and then add its feed to their aggregator.

If you opt not to generate an RSS feed for you blog, then those who exclusively use readers are unlikely to follow your blog closely. This puts you at a significant disadvantage relative to your competition.

#45: Truncate Your RSS Feeds to Hook Readers

With tip #44 in mind, it is always a good idea to try to hook readers when possible. Rather than simply allow them to gain all of the information from the reader without re-visiting your site, you should consider truncating your RSS feed.

Truncating your RSS feed at a certain amount of characters will prevent people from reading the entire message through their reader. Instead, they will get hooked by your catchy opening line, but will then have to visit your site if they want to get the entire blog post.

#46: Add a 'Find Us Elsewhere' Box

In addition to pulling people from social media sites and directing them to your website, you should also think about doing the reverse: taking people who visit your website and getting them to follow you on social media sites. This might seem counterintuitive at first (after all, don't you want everyone to eventually end up on sales pages?), but in fact, it can be a highly profitable approach. The reason for this is that it increases customer/visitor engagement, which ultimately translates into more contact and then more sales.

One way in which you can employ this strategy is by adding a "Find Us Elsewhere" box on your website. This is a small box on your site that contains icons that link to your profile pages on Twitter, Facebook, and other sites. By clicking these links, visitors can quickly scan your content and decide whether or not they want to follow you or become your friend/fan.

#47: Use Disqus with Tumblr

One of the things that many people find off-putting about blogs is that they have to create profiles to comment on them. Fortunately, when it comes to using a service such as Tumblr, you can allow people to comment without creating a new account.

How is this? Instead of creating a Tumblr account to comment, you can configure your account to use Disqus.com to allow visitors to login using accounts for which they already have profiles.

For instance, if your visitors already have Facebook or Twitter accounts, they can login using their credentials for those sites. They can then post comments that are linked with those identities. Of course, if they don't want to be identified, they can also post comments as guests.

#48: Use Disqus to Allow Site Comments

In addition to using Disqus with your Tumblr blog, you can also use it for your site in general. This can be very useful, as it will allow visitors to post a range of comments about your website. This can help you to get feedback faster; and to respond to it faster. It will also allow you to use your visitors to generate content for your site.

The following are some good uses for Disqus on your site:

1. Ask visitors to leave feedback about your site, so that you can make corresponding changes.
2. Ask visitors to post product ideas, so that you can capture repeated suggestions and use them to guide your development plans.
3. Ask visitors to post testimonials and product reviews, so that you can use them to promote your products.

Of course, whenever you open up your site up to free commenting, you put yourself at risk of having inappropriate or negative comments being posted on your site. For this reason, you may want to either police the comments carefully; or set them up so that they need to be approved before they are posted.

#49: Create a Discussion Forum for Your Website

Another excellent way to get people to engage the content on your site and to revisit it frequently is to create a forum. Many hosting services now allow you to do this with a plugin. From there, you can simply manage the site through the control panel, adding forums, managing sticky notes, and deleting posts as necessary.

Of course, creating and managing a forum can be a tricky process. And it is important for you to understand that it is unlikely that your forum will be successful unless you dedicate a significant amount of time to the launch phase.

Without dedicating this time to your site, it will be hard to get it to go from a "ghost forum," where no one posts to a forum where there is lively activity (and where it is mentioned on other sites).

#50: Populate Your Discussion Forum

Although it may seem like a lot of work, launching your discussion forum is only the start. It's a pre-requisite for one day having a populous forum, but it is by no means sufficient for creating a good forum. In fact, most forums start and end as ghost forums because their owners never take the time to populate them.

If you want your forum to be successful, you will have to take the time to populate it with individuals who will engage in lively discussions; and who will perpetuate your forum by mentioning it elsewhere.

There are several ways in which you can do this. I've listed some below:

1. Create threads on the forum about important topics in your niche. Since new visitors will find that the forum is empty, they will be hesitant to post; however, if there is at least one other person posting threads, they may take the time to respond.

3. 2. Pull forum members from blogs and forums. Find places where individuals already engage in active discussions; and solicit them for your forum indirectly. You can do this by including a signature with your forum and blog posts that links to your forum.

Overall, remember that if you want to retain your forum members, you will have to keep them engaged. So, as you step up your promotion efforts, remember to simultaneously scale up your on-forum engagement efforts.

#51: Make Money from Your Discussion Forum

Once you have created a successful forum, which has both "core" members and lurkers, it is time to start figuring out how to reap a return on your investment. Try adopting one or more of the following three strategies:

1. Use a service like Adsense to place pay-per-click ads on your forum.

2. Use the forum to announce product launches and to promote sales.

3. Use the forum to promote your products through permanent threads.

Alternatively, you might consider using your forum to answer any questions about your products.

#52: Create Your Own Social Network

In addition to participating in existing social networks, some entrepreneurs choose to start their own niche social networks. In the past, this was quite difficult to do; however, today, there are pieces of software that make it easy to do this.

One such piece of software can be found at www.phpfox.com. It makes creating social networks relatively easy; and allows you to do so entirely through a user-friendly control panel. Although there are many products that now allow you to do this, phpfox is one of the best and allows a great deal of customization.

Before you venture into creating your own social network, it is probably a good idea to spend some time thinking about whether this approach is compatible with your current business; and whether you can come up with a good strategy to monetize it in the long run.

#53: Populate Your Social Network

There are several good ways in which you can populate your social network. I've listed some of these below:

1.   Try to capture members for your network from larger, non-niche networks, such as Facebook. You can do this by seeking out people who look like good matches for your network; and then casually exposing them to the network, so that they can decide whether or not to use it.
2.   Use Twitter to draw members into your network. Since your Twitter marketing campaign will revolve around capturing people who already work in your niche, most of the people who are following you on Twitter will already be good matches for your network.
3.   Search for new members on blogs in your network; and capture them by commenting and including a signature.

#54: Generate Revenue from Your Social Network

The final question you must ask is how to generate revenue from your social network. One obvious route is to use it to channel traffic to your products, since most of its members will already have a vested interest in your niche.

Another possibility is to generate revenue by selling ad space on your site. You can do this directly by selling banner ads, text ads, and other ad space. Alternatively, you can do this indirectly by inserting Adsense code into your website.

#55: Promote New Products Using Twitter

One useful way in which you can employ Twitter is to promote new products. It's important to note that the bulk of your tweets should be high-quality, free information about your niche; however, when you have a new product available, you should also tweet to let people know about the upcoming launch.

In fact, it might not be a bad idea to create a site page with a countdown to the launch date. You can then use that page to post periodic updates about the product and its features. You can also direct your Twitter users to that page.

#56: Using Twitter to Promote a Special Offer

In addition to promoting your new products through Twitter, you can also use it to promote a special offer. You can do this by bundling together a bunch of your products, reducing the price drastically, and then creating a sales page. You can then tweet about it to let your followers know that you are offering a one-time steep discount.

#57: Use Twitter to Grow Your Email List

Earlier, I mentioned that you can use your email list to grow your Twitter follower list and your Facebook fan base. However, you can also do the reverse: you can use Twitter to grow your email list. You can then use this list to sell products.

If you don't already have a mailing list, that's a good place to start. Setup an autoresponder using Aweber. Create an introduction mailing series that includes several product pitches, and then begin capturing subscribers.

Once you have setup your autoresponder, you can announce this on Twitter, so that your followers know that they can get free, useful content through a free subscription.

#58: Create a Wordpress Blog

If you're not thrilled by the simplicity that blogger and Tumblr offer, then you may want to consider a more robust blogging platform. As I mentioned earlier, Wordpress is an excellent alternative. It has a large range of plugins and themes.

If you do decide to start a Wordpress blog, I personally recommend installing the All in One SEO plugin for starters. After you do that, it's a good idea to begin filling your blog with relevant content. You can do this by hiring a ghost-writer to create your blog entries for you.

#59: Use Your Page to Send Out Information

Another benefit of having a Facebook page is that you can send out information to your fans easily. If you followed my earlier tip of contacting your autoresponder course subscribers and getting them to become a fan on Facebook, then you should now have a broad base of fans to contact.

You can make use of this situation by sending them information about your business, such as dates of sales, coupons, and upcoming product launch information.

#60: Request Information Using Your Page

In addition to sending out information from your page, you can also use it to gather information from your followers, as I've mentioned previously. In particular, there are three things that you should try to recover from your followers: =

1. Survey data about your business. If you can get your followers to fill out surveys about your products (perhaps by offering some incentives), you have a good chance of capturing vital information that you can use to create, market, and fix your products.
2. Photos or art related to your business. In many cases this simply isn't applicable, but in others, it is; and can be one of your greatest assets. If you can get your followers to post pictures of themselves using your products, this can be a very useful way to draw in additional people on Facebook.

3. Testimonials. Regardless of what business you are in, testimonials can play a vital role in improving your credibility. For this reason, you should make a concerted effort to get testimonials from your customers through Facebook.

#61: Use Event Invitations on Facebook

There are many ways in which you can support a product launch through Facebook; however, I personally recommend that you do so by creating an event. You can then promote the event by inviting all of your business's "fans" to participate in the event (i.e. your product launch).

It's important that you spell out exactly what it means to participate in the launch event. For instance, you might explain that on the launch date, you are going to hold a variety of contests and award prizes, ranging from cash awards to coupons for products.

Additionally, it is important to explain to fans that they must confirm that they are attending the event in order to be eligible to receive prizes in the contests. This will create a buzz about your event; and possibly encourage new people to become fans.

#62: Create a Facebook Application

In many situations, this simply won't apply to you, as it does not make sense for most businesses to create an application on Facebook; however, if you happen to have the right business model, an application could be a great way to increase your business's presence on Facebook.

If you don't know anything about creating applications, don't worry. You don't actually have to program the application yourself. Rather, you can simply work through the following steps:

1. Draft a plan for your application. Think about the purpose of your application; and how you want your fans to interact with it. Or do you want it to serve some other purpose?
2. Review your plan; and clean it up, so that someone who knows nothing about your project can understand it.

3. Post your product on Elance.com; and allow programmers to bid on it. If you get offers that are at, or below your budget, consider taking them if the bidder has a sufficiently strong portfolio.

If you work through this process, you should be able to get a good app at a reasonable price. From there, it will be up to you to promote it; and to get it to catch on.

#63: Create a Free Discussion Forum

As I mentioned previously, one of the best ways to drive traffic to your site is by creating a forum; and then channelling that forum traffic to your site. One way you can do this easily and for free is to create your forum on your Facebook page.

The Facebook app; 'forum for pages' can be applied to your page using the usual method through gaining your permission. Once applied you can then start adding various different topics and posts. Another way it can be used is for demonstration and even training purposes.

If you are using Wordpress then there are many forum plugins available. However 'Mingle Forum' is a simple plugin that is easy to set up and configure in around 5 minutes. You then have a forum on your Wordpress site or blog fully installed..

#64: Include a 'Welcome' Page with Offers

Another thing you can do once you have a page ready is to change the default setting for people who visit it. Frequently, businesses and organizations will leave their "info" or "wall" pages as the default arrival page; however, one recent trend is to make a 'Welcome' page as your default page.

This 'Welcome' page can include a variety of different things, such as coupons, news, sales information, and product inventory information.

#65: Cross-Promote Your Social Media Accounts

As a rule of thumb, it is always a good idea to cross-promote your social media marketing campaigns. This will increase your exposure in both campaigns; and can help to increase your customer engagement.

#66: Create a Twitter Contest

One recent trend in social media is to create "re-tweeting" contests. The idea behind these is both simple and brilliant. If used correctly, they can generate a tidal wave of new followers for your Twitter account.

In short, here's what you need to do: start by coming up with a sufficiently desirable contest prize. This might be something like £50, free products, or a gift card. Once you've done this, announce you will be giving away this prize for free via a raffle; however, in order to enter the raffle, a person must a) be a follower; and b) must re-tweet your contest announcement.

The idea behind this, as I've said, is simple: each entrant in your contest will re-tweet to tens, hundreds, or even thousands of followers. The followers of your followers will see the re-tweet, become your follower; and then re-tweet to others.

#67: Create iPhone Applications for Your Feeds

As I've mentioned before, some of these tips are broadly applicable, while others are not. This tip may not be applicable for many businesses, but not for others.

The idea here is to create an iPhone application that showcases your social media campaigns. For instance, you could create an app that allows people who download it to follow your blog RSS feed, see your tweets, and view your Facebook update status. It could also include a calendar for your business that provides product, sales, and coupon updates.

It's important to note that you don't need any programming experience in order to create such an app. You can do it using a program such as the following: http://www.taplynx.com/.

#68: Modify your iPhone Application for Use with other Smartphones

Once you've completed your iPhone application, the next step is to modify it, so that you can also give it away for free for use on other platforms, such as Palm OS, Windows, and Android.

In many cases, programs that allow you to create applications using a drag-and-drop interface will also allow you to create versions for multiple platforms. In this case, the process will be relatively simple.

If this is not the case, then you may want to consider hiring a programmer to make the adjustments, so that you introduce your application in other platforms. You can do this by finding someone on Elance.

86

#69: Promote Website Updates Using Twitter

Another good use of Twitter is to promote recent updates to your website. In this case, you don't have to say anything blatantly commercial. Instead, you can simply point out that your site has been updated; and mention that followers should check it out and let you know what they think.

#70: Add Digg/Reddit Buttons to Your Website

As I mentioned before, it's always a good idea to try to get your customers and site visitors to follow you on Facebook and Twitter. It is also a good idea to try to get them to help promote your business through sites like Digg and Reddit. For this reason, you may want to include a button on your blog posts and on your site pages that allows visitors to "Digg It," so that you receive votes for your site on social bookmarking sites (and, thus, rank better).

#71: Add Social Network Share Buttons

Another thing you may want to consider doing is adding a "tweet this" and/or "post this to my Facebook account" button to your blog posts. This will make it easier for visitors to promote your site to their friends and family members, which will ultimately benefit you.

#72: Use YouTube to Talk to Your Customers

Earlier, we talked about using YouTube to offer a tutorial series to your visitors and customers. Another good use of YouTube is to make live announcements. This is not for everyone, but if you decide to use it, it has the potential to lend a significant amount of credibility to your business.

Before you whip out the webcam and get to work, first spend some time planning out your video. What do you want to communicate and how do you want to organize your message? These are important things to ask and answer before delivering a scatterbrained or confusing video message.

#73: Using the "Insights" Feature on Facebook

One often-ignored feature of Facebook pages is the "insight" feature. This will allow you to break-down your fan site traffic in great detail, including the location, IP addresses, likes and dislikes, and other details about your fan site traffic. This can prove extremely useful if you are trying to analyse your visitors to determine what types of people buy your product and have an interest in your niche.

#74: Promote Your Photos and Testimonials

Another way in which you can use your Facebook page is to promote fan photos and testimonials. As I mentioned earlier, you should make a concerted effort to extract testimonials, photos, and relevant artwork from your customers and visitors.

Once you get it, add it to your Facebook page (if they'll allow it). This will provide you with some evidence that you are running a legitimate business and selling a good product, so that people will be more willing to accept your friend invites and join your fan page.

#75: Promote Your Facebook Page with a Facebook Ad

Once you have your page in place, consider promoting it with a Facebook ad. Since Facebook can capture a tremendous amount of demographic information about its users (because they freely post it in their profiles), you can drill down carefully to determine which types of profiles your ads should be placed near.

This is both an inexpensive and highly-targeted strategy for bolstering the ranks of your page; and I highly suggest that you do it to get the ball rolling.

#76: Add a Google+ Button to Your Site

Just as you added a "Find Us Elsewhere" box, you may also want to consider integrating Google + into your marketing strategy. You can do this by allowing people who visit your site and see something they like to automatically post it to their Google+ account.

 If you're unfamiliar with Google+, create an email account at Gmail.com and then spend some time exploring the different areas of the network which includes among other features; you're 'Stream.' As this suggests this gives updates from your followers.

'Circles' each person you connect with is placed in a circle e.g. acquaintances or family members.

'Hangouts' is where you can invite members of your circles to join you for an online chat either 1-2-1 or in a group.

#77: Start Conversations to Get Readers Involved

Finally, as a general rule of thumb, it is always important to get the conversation started, no matter what form of social media you are using. Whether you're firing off @reply on Twitter or discussing some important topic on your Facebook page forum, it is important to take the initiative to get people involved.

When you first start your social media marketing efforts, the only person who will be invested in your business is you. You must accept this; and understand that growing your network of followers is ultimately your responsibility and no one else's. If you do a good job, the responsibility will slowly shift over time from you to people who will become heavily invested in your network and will want to play a role in perpetuating it.

Conclusion

Over the course of this report, we've gone over 77 different strategies for employing social media services to grow your customer base, to market your products, to come up with new product ideas, and to collect information about your visitors.

Throughout this report, we've gone from general suggestions about social media etiquette to specific suggestions about how to use certain social media tools. We've also discussed how to create your own social networks and populate them if you believe this will be a good option for your business.

Now that you've read all of this, take some time to process it, make plans accordingly; and then jump in. Don't make the mistake that many other businesses make of waiting and worrying. Instead, get to work building your social media empire; and use it to generate massive flows of income for your business.

Success Stories

"I have a website and online advertising which I thought was working quite well; that is until I met Ian! He totally restructured my online marketing, focussing on the social networking site facebook. I must admit I hadn't tapped into the power of facebook as a marketing tool, but Ian has built me a fantastic page which I can update, edit and share with everyone on facebook enabling me to attract new business. The information Ian shared with me was easy to follow and seeing the page up and running has boosted my business profile and added some very valuable clients already!"

Dave Porter Photography, Peterborough

" Big Thanks to Ian who has guided me every step of the way through what can seem like the overwhelming world of social media marketing! Ian's support, knowledge and encouragement opened my eyes to the possibilities and opportunities that can be gained through social media.

Social media has certainly increased traffic to my website resulting in greater product exposure, brand awareness and most importantly a large client database that without social media would have taken years to build up. With Ian's expertise and his ability to translate 'techy jargon' into plain English, I have been able to take my business to the next level and have the edge over my competitors. Thank You Ian!"

Lisa Peacock, Lisa Jane Bridal, Cambridge.

"Just thought I would put in words how helpful Ian has been to our business.

We run busy clothing wholesalers with many of our customers coming to us via our website. Ian has shown us how social media can completely change the way we market our goods and we are so grateful to him. As well as writing a comprehensive social media strategy, he explained to my staff many easy to use techniques that I am sure will help us interact with our customers professionally and profitably for years to come!

Thanks Ian."

Laurence Sugarman. Owner, Eles Clothing, Nottingham.

Closing Thoughts

So now you have 77 tips that you can take and integrate into your social media strategy to help promote your business.

Most of these tips are simple to implement, however others may take a little more effort and technical know-how, so think carefully about which ones you choose to use.

Let Me Know How You Get On

It would be great if you would let me know how you get on with implementing these tips.

Please feel free to visit my website and leave me a message, and maybe we can let everyone know of the successful results that you have achieved.

You will also find on there a link to all the resources listed in this book, along with a link to download a complimentary copy of 'Twitter Boom.' Which is a comprehensive guide on how to use Twitter to grow your following and your business.

http://www.igmediamarketing.com

Workshops and Consultancy

I run a number of workshops throughout the year covering the many different areas of social media marketing, and have also been asked to speak at events in the UK.

Please feel free to contact me on the email address below if you would like a complimentary, informal chat about your social media marketing campaign.

If you would like me to speak at your event, or run a workshop for your company please don't hesitate to contact me by email; ian@igmediamarketing.com